My Pocket Guide

Massachusetts

By Carole Marsh

Correlates with Massachusetts Curriculum Framework — **MCF**

THE **MASSACHUSETTS** ExperiencE

The GALLOPADE GANG

Carole Marsh
Bob Longmeyer
Chad Beard
Cecil Anderson
Steven Saint-Laurent
Karin Petersen

Jill Sanders
Kathy Zimmer
Terry Briggs
Pat Newman
Billie Walburn
Jackie Clayton

Pam Dufresne
Cranston Davenport
Lisa Stanley
Antoinette Miller
Victoria DeJoy
Al Fortunatti
Shery Kearney

Published by GALLOPADE INTERNATIONAL

www.massachusettsexperience.com
800-536-2GET • www.gallopade.com

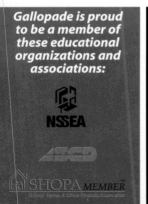

Gallopade is proud to be a member of these educational organizations and associations:

NSSEA

ASCD

SHOPA MEMBER
School, Home, & Office Products Association

Other Massachusetts Experience Products

- The Massachusetts Experience!
- The BIG Massachusetts Reproducible Activity Book
- The Massachusetts Coloring Book
- My First Book About Massachusetts!
- Massachusetts "Jography": A Fun Run Through Our State
- Massachusetts Jeopardy!: Answers and Questions About Our State
- The Massachusetts Experience! Sticker Pack
- The Massachusetts Experience! Poster/Map
- Discover Massachusetts CD-ROM
- Massachusetts "Geo" Bingo Game
- Massachusetts "Histo" Bingo Game

A Word From the Author... (okay, a few words)...

Hi!

Here's your own handy pocket guide about the great state of Massachusetts! It really will fit in a pocket—I tested it. And it really will be useful when you want to know a fact you forgot, to bone up for a test, or when your teacher says, "I wonder . . ." and you have the answer—instantly! Wow, I'm impressed!

Get smart, have fun!
Carole Marsh

Massachusetts Basics explores your state's symbols and their special meanings!

Massachusetts Geography digs up the what's where in your state!

Massachusetts History is like traveling through time to some of your state's great moments!

Massachusetts People introduces you to famous personalities and your next-door neighbors!

Massachusetts Places shows you where you might enjoy your next family vacation!

Massachusetts Nature - no preservatives here, just what Mother Nature gave to Massachusetts!

All the real fun stuff that we just HAD to save for its own section!

Massachusetts Basics

Massachusetts Geography

Massachusetts History

Massachusetts People

Massachusetts Places

Massachusetts Nature

Massachusetts Miscellany

Who Named You?

Massachusetts' official state name is...

the Commonwealth of Massachusetts

State Name

COMMONWEALTH: a nation or state governed by the people; from the word "commonweal," meaning "for the public."

Statehood: February 6, 1788

Massachusetts was the 6th state to ratify the United States Constitution and join the Union.

Massachusetts was the first state to be on a state-commemorative quarter in the year 2000. Look for it in cash registers everywhere!

Coccinella noemnotata is my name (that's Latin for ladybug)! What's YOURS?

What's In A Name?

Massachusetts got its name from the Massachuset Indian tribe. The name means "large hill place" or "near the great hill." The Great Blue Hill outside of Boston is what may have inspired the Indians to choose this name. The Massachuset lived in the Massachusetts Bay area which extends from Cape Ann in the north to Plymouth in the south.

Many of Massachusetts' city names, such as Boston and Plymouth, reflect its English heritage.

WHO Are You Calling Names?

State Nicknames

Massachusetts is not the only name by which our state is recognized. Like many other states, Massachusetts has some nicknames, official or unofficial!

Old Colony State

Baked Bean State

Puritan State

Bay State

Plymouth Colony was the first English settlement in Massachusetts and later became part of the Massachusetts Bay Colony as more people came to the New World.

State Capital:
Boston

State Capital/ Capitol

Since 1630, Boston has been a center for government and economics in Massachusetts. It was originally settled by Governor Winthrop from England along with 150 Puritans. He realized Boston would become a major seaport as it still is today. Boston was incorporated as a city in 1822.

The newest State House was originally designed by Charles Bullfinch in 1795. It is considered the crowning glory of Beacon Hill. It has a golden dome and the building sits on what was once the pasture land of John Hancock.

Word Definition

CAPITAL: a town or city that is the official seat of government
CAPITOL: the building in which the government officials meet

7

State Government

Who's in Charge Here?

Massachusetts' GOVERNMENT has three branches:

EXECUTIVE	LEGISLATIVE	JUDICIAL

State Government

A governor, lieutenant governor, and eight elected councillors, secretary of state, attorney general, state treasurer, and state auditor	The legislative branch is officially called the General Court Two Houses: Senate (40 members) House of Representatives (160 members)	Supreme Judicial Court (a chief justice and six associate judges) Superior Court (a chief justice and sixty-six associate judges) Trial Courts

Although most bills originate in the senate or house of representatives, any citizen may file a bill through a legislator. This is the right of free petition that exists in the state of Massachusetts.

When you are 18 and register according to Massachusetts laws, you can vote! So please do! Your vote counts!

State
Flag

Massachusetts' current state flag was adopted in 1971. It features the state coat of arms on a field of white on both sides of the flag.

As you travel throughout Massachusetts, count the times you see the Massachusetts flag! Look for it on government vehicles, too!

State Seal

The state seal of Massachusetts is of circular design with "Seal of the Republic of Massachusetts" in Latin on the edge. Inside is the coat of arms which is a blue shield with a five pointed star symbolizing that Massachusetts was one of the original thirteen states. A Native American is holding a bow in one hand and in the other hand an arrow pointing down to signify peace. The state motto is written on a blue ribbon at the bottom of the shield.

State Seal & Motto

Word Definition

MOTTO: a sentence, phrase, or word expressing the spirit or purpose of an organization or group

State Motto

Massachusetts' state motto is...

The state seal of Massachusetts is the oldest symbol of the state dating back to 1780.

Ense petit placidam sub libertate quietem.

It means "By the sword we seek peace but peace only under liberty."

Birds of a Feather

Black-capped chickadees are cheerful birds and can be identified by their call: "chick-adee-dee-dee." They are also called dickeybirds, titmouses, and tomtits. The bird's markings are gray, black, and light brown with white cheeks.

State Bird

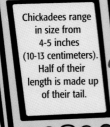

Chickadees range in size from 4-5 inches (10-13 centimeters). Half of their length is made up of their tail.

AMERICAN ELM

Woodman, spare that tree! —George Pope Morris

The American Elm is sometimes called the White Elm. One tree can have over a million leaves! They grow to be 80–120 feet (24–37 meters) in height. The number of these trees in our country has declined due to Dutch Elm disease. The American Elm was chosen to commemorate an elm on Cambridge Square where General Washington took command of the Continental Army in 1775.

State Flower

A lovelier flower on earth was never sown. — William Wordsworth

The state flower is the Mayflower and is also called the trailing arbutus and ground laurel. It has five small pink or white petals and a sweet fragrance. The Mayflower likes to grow in evergreen woods or in sandy or rocky soil. It was adopted as a state emblem on May 1, 1918.

The Mayflower is now on the endangered species list because it has become very scarce.

RIDDLE:
If the state flower got mixed up with the state bird, what would you have?

ANSWER: A chickadee that sailed on the Mayflower!—it could happen!

13

A Whale of a Tale!

State
Marine
Mammal

The Right Whale is the state marine mammal. Its habitat is the northern oceans. It can range in length from 50–60 feet (15–18 meters). It does not have a dorsal (back) fin like some whales. At one time whales were an important part of the economy for Massachusetts' colonists. Whale oil, whalebone, and other whale by-products played an important role in people's lives. Whales were hunted so much that they almost became extinct. The whale population is slowly increasing now that whale watching has replaced whale hunting!

Whale oil lamps were in common use until petroleum was discovered in 1800s.

THE "KING" WHELK!
THE NEW ENGLAND NEPTUNE

State Shell

The New England Neptune belongs to the whelk family. The shells can grow from finger size to hand size or even bigger. The ones found on the coast of Massachusetts are drab in color, mostly gray or white. The snails live in these shells. Egg capsules are laid by the female snail. When the eggs hatch, the larvae swim away. Snails are carnivores and like to eat oysters, other bivalves, and dead fish and crabs.

Gee, the next time I go to the beach, I hope I don't end up as a snack for some snail!

Whelk egg capsules were used by some sailors to clean their hands. Sea wash balls!

The Square Dance

The square dance is an American folk dance related to the English country dance and French ballroom dance. It includes squares, rounds, clogging, contra line, the Virginia reel, and heritage dances.

The dancers move in pairs or sets to lively music played on fiddles or other instruments. A caller announces the steps of the country dance.

Boston is referred to as the Athens of America because it is a cultural center for ballet, concerts, plays, and the other arts.

State Berries

From the Bog to your Table!

State Berries

It was the Native Americans, the Wampanoag, who introduced cranberries to the Pilgrims. Cranberries grow on vines in wet, spongy ground called bogs. At harvest time the bogs are flooded, the water is churned, and the berries fall off the vines. As they float in the water, they are gathered for processing. Massachusetts produces about 200 million pounds (90 million kilograms) of cranberries each year!

If all the cranberries grown in a year were strung together, they would circle the earth at least 30 times!

17

Plymouth Rock

State
Historic
Rock

In 1620, the Pilgrims came ashore to a place they called Plymouth Colony. They did not actually land on the rock, but this place where they first stepped into the New World, has always been called Plymouth Rock. It is a symbol for all Americans of our country's humble beginnings. The state legislature, wishing to honor the Pilgrims, named Plymouth Rock a state historical symbol. Many tourists come each year to view the rock and to commemorate where the Pilgrims landed.

The Mayflower was only 106 feet (32 meters) in length. The voyage lasted 65 days carrying 102 English passengers and crew plus all their possessions.

I would be as snug as a bug in a rug!

LADY BUG, LADY BUG...

State Insect

Lady bugs are usually red with black spots, but they can be yellow or orange, too. They belong to the beetle family. Lady bugs eat aphids and mites. Farmers are always glad to have them around to protect their crops from these pests. Second grade children chose the lady bug as the state insect!

Lady bugs hibernate in the winter by clustering together in large swarms.

Wow! I got top billing in this book!

19

Atlantic Cod— Colonial Heroes

State Fish

In 1784, the colonists hung a gilded codfish in the Massachusetts State House to recognize the importance of this fish to their survival during early New England settlement. It is still there today! The average cod weighs 10–25 pounds (4.5–11 kilograms). Cod like to eat mollusks, crabs, starfish, worms, squid and small fish. About 83 million cod are caught each year. They often move south for the winter to spawn. Large females can produce three to five million eggs!

Massachusetts "Sacred Cod"
Put a cod filet on foil. Drizzle with lemon juice. Sprinkle with salt and pepper. Add shredded smoked ham and broil fish until done. Small cod cut into strips for cooking is called Scrod.

Sounds fishy to me!

The State of
Massachusetts

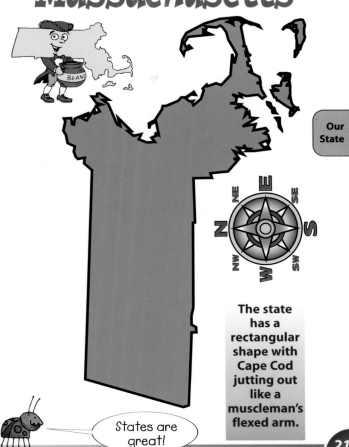

Our State

The state has a rectangular shape with Cape Cod jutting out like a muscleman's flexed arm.

States are great!

21

State Location

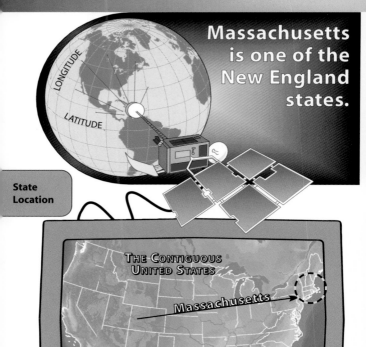

Massachusetts is one of the New England states.

LONGITUDE

LATITUDE

State Location

THE CONTIGUOUS UNITED STATES

Massachusetts

Word Definition

LATITUDE: Imaginary lines which run horizontally east and west around the globe
LONGITUDE: Imaginary lines which run vertically north and south around the globe

These border Massachusetts:

States: New Hampshire, Vermont, New York, Connecticut, and Rhode Island

Bodies of water: Atlantic Ocean, Massachusetts Bay, Cape Cod Bay, Buzzards Bay, Nantucket Sound

State Neighbors

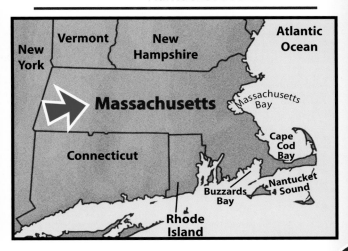

I'll Take the Low Road...

Massachusetts stretches 113 miles (182 kilometers) from north to south—or south to north. Either way, it's a long drive!

East-West, North-South, Area

Total Area: Approximately 9,241 square miles (23,932 square kilometers)

Land Area: Approximately 7,838 square miles (20,299 square kilometers)

Massachusetts is 183 miles (295 kilometers) from east to west—or west to east. Either way, it's *still* a long drive!

This is a compass rose. It helps you find the right direction on a map!

You Take the High Road!

HIGHEST POINT
MOUNT GREYLOCK—3,487 FEET (1,064 METERS)

The Taconic Mountains are very rugged and have an average height of 2,000 feet (600 meters). Mount Greylock is located here. The Berkshire Hills provide some of the loveliest scenery in the state. The Berkshires average about 2,500 feet (760 meters) in height and offer a great area for skiing in the winter months.

LOWEST POINT
SEA LEVEL ALONG THE ATLANTIC OCEAN

I'm County-ing on You!

Massachusetts is divided into 14 counties.

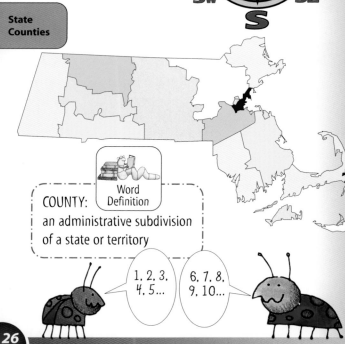

COUNTY:

Word Definition

an administrative subdivision of a state or territory

1, 2, 3, 4, 5...

6, 7, 8, 9, 10...

Natural Resources

It's All Natural!

Forests cover 55 percent of the land in Massachusetts.

Word Definition

NATURAL RESOURCES: things that exist in or are formed by nature

Minerals and rocks:

granite
limestone
marble
peat
sand
gravel
sandstone

Rock and Roll!

Massachusetts is a leading commercial fishing state. Besides cod, crabs, clams, squid, and other seafood are available.

27

Weather, Or Not?!

Massachusetts' temperatures can drop to 25°F (-4°C) in the winter and reach 71°F (22°C) in the summer.

"Nor'easters" are violent storms or hurricanes occurring along the New England coast during the late summer and fall. In winter these storms can be blizzards.

Weather

Highest temperature: 107°F (42°C), at New Bedford and Chester on August 2, 1975

°F=Degrees Fahrenheit °C=Degrees Celsius

Lowest temperature: -34°F (-37°C), at Birch Hill Dam on January 18, 1957

In 1978, a blizzard dumped 2–4 feet (61–121 centimeters) of snow over the entire state of Massachusetts.

Topography

BACK ON TOP

Massachusetts' topography includes the Coastal Lowlands, covering more than a third of the state stretching inland from the coast. The New England Upland is made up of hills and includes the Connecticut River Valley which has very fertile land for farming. The Taconic Range and the Berkshire Hills are part of the Appalachian Mountain Range and are found in the western portion of the state.

Word Definition

TOPOGRAPHY: the detailed mapping of the features of a small area or district

Massachusetts is called the "Bay State" because of all the bays found along the Coastal Lowland.

Sea Level

100 m 328 ft

200 m 656 ft

500 m 1,640 ft

1,000 m 3,281 ft

2,000 m 6,562 ft

5,000 m 16,404 ft

Topography

King of the Hill

Appalachian Mountain Range: Taconic Range including Mount Greylock, the Berkshire Hills

Drumlins are rolling hills found near the coast. They were shaped by the glaciers that once covered the land.

Climb every mountain..

Down The River

Here are some of Massachusetts' major rivers:

- **Connecticut River**
- **Charles River**
- **Mystic River**
- **Neponset River**
- **Merrimack River**
- **Housatonic River**

The USS *Constitution*, our country's first warship, is docked on the Charles River in Charlestown Harbor.

Grab a paddle!

Gone Fishin'

Major Lakes

Major ponds and reservoirs in Massachusetts include:

- **Assawompsett Pond**
- **North Watuppa Pond**
- **Long Pond**
- **Walden Pond**
- **Quabbin Reservoir**
- **Wachusett Reservoir**
- **East Brimfield Reservoir**
- **Cobble Mountain Reservoir**

Lake Chargoggagoggmanchuaggagoggchaubunagungamaug has the longest place name in the state.
It is Nipmuc for "You fish your side of the lake. I fish my side. Nobody fishes the middle."

Word Definition

RESERVOIR: a body of water stored for public use

ARE YOU A CITY MOUSE... OR A COUNTRY MOUSE?

English colonists named many cities and towns after places in England.

Have you heard of these wonderful Massachusetts town, city, or crossroad names? Perhaps you can start your own list!

Cities & Towns

MAJOR CITIES:
- Boston
- Brockton
- Fall River
- Lynn
- Gloucester
- Worcester
- Lowell
- New Bedford
- Springfield
- Pittsfield
- Fitchburg

SMALLER TOWNS
- Northampton
- Holyoke
- Princeton
- Amherst
- Hatfield
- Hadley
- Framingham
- Salem
- Sturbridge
- Hyannis Port
- Edgartown

Is that so they wouldn't feel lonesome for their homeland?

Transportation

Major Interstate Highways

Interstates: I-95, I-495, I-90, I-91, I-190, I-290, I-195

Railroads

Massachusetts has about 1,650 miles (2,660 kilometers) of railroad tracks linking not only state cities, but also connecting to out of state urban centers.

Transpor-tation

Major Airports

Logan International Airport in Boston is the largest and busiest airport in the state. There are many smaller airports including private airfields, as well.

Seaports

Boston is a major seaport city in the New England region. Ferries serve Nantucket Island and Martha's Vineyard carrying passengers and cars. The Cape Cod Canal is part of the Intracoastal Waterway and allows oceangoing ships to go from New England to the Middle Atlantic states along a shorter route.

Public transportation in Boston is called the "T" and includes subway, trolley, bus, and commuter rail lines.

Timeline

1500s	Algonquian tribes live in the Massachusetts area	
1620	Pilgrims arrive on the Mayflower and found Plymouth Colony	
1621	Pilgrims celebrate the first Thanksgiving	
1630	Puritans found Massachusetts Bay Colony at Boston	
1636	Harvard is established in New Towne (Cambridge)	
1692	Witch hunts and witchcraft trials disrupt Salem	
1767	England passes Townshend Acts, taxing tea, glass, lead, and paint coming into the colonies	
1770	Colonists are killed during the Boston Massacre	
1773	Boston Tea Party takes place when colonists dump British tea into Boston Harbor to protest the tea tax	
1775	Paul Revere rides to warn the colonists of British attack	
1776	Massachusetts approves the Declaration of Independence	
1786–87	Shay's Rebellion	**Timeline**
1788	Massachusetts becomes the sixth state to enter the Union	
1837	Mount Holyoke College is the first women's college founded in the U.S.	
1897	Boston opens nation's first subway; first Boston Marathon is run	
1917	About 198,000 people from Massachusetts serve during World War I	
1941–45	About half a million Massachusetts men and women serve in World War II	
1960	John Fitzgerald Kennedy is elected 35th president of the U.S.	
1988	Massachusetts is 200 years old	
1990	The Bay state population grows to over six million	
1997	The USS *Constitution* (*Old Ironsides*) sails under her own canvas for the first time in 116 years	

On to the 21st Century!

Here come the humans!

Thousands of years ago, ancient peoples inhabited Massachusetts. They may have originally come across a frozen bridge of land between Asia and Alaska. If so, they slowly traveled east until some settled in what would one day become the state of Massachusetts.

In 1614, around 30,000 Native Americans lived here. Disease brought by the white colonists caused their population to decline.

Native Americans Once Ruled!

The Algonquian tribes living in Massachusetts were the Massachuset, Nauset, Nipmuc, Pennacook, Pocumtuc, and the Wampanoag. Their societies were well-ordered, and they had tools and methods of hunting that were very effective for their needs. Dugout boats were their means of transportation on water. The Native Americans hunted deer, gathered nuts and berries, and caught seafood.

Early Indians

Friendly Native Americans like Squanto helped Pilgrims survive their first winter by teaching them to fish and plant corn. Samoset introduced the Pilgrims to Massasoit, the Wampanoag leader. The Pilgrims and Indians signed a peace treaty promising to protect each other if they were attacked. In the fall of 1621, the first Thanksgiving was celebrated between the colonists and the Native Americans.

Land Ho!

The first explorers to visit Massachusetts may have been the Vikings around the year 1000. In 1498, John Cabot sailed along the coast of Massachusetts while looking for a route to Asia.

Giovanni da Verazzano, an Italian explorer sailing under the French flag, traced the coastline.

Exploration

In 1602, Bartholomew Gosnold, an English captain, arrived in the area. He named Cape Cod after all the codfish that were there. Other explorers between 1603–1609 who came to investigate the region were: Martin Pring, George Waymouth, Samuel de Champlain, Henry Hudson, and Adriaen Block.

In 1614, Captain John Smith mapped the Massachusetts Bay area naming many of the places there. He described Massachusetts as a paradise in his book, *A Description of New England.*

European countries were interested in the New World for various reasons. Gold was often a lure to draw explorers there. Furs and plentiful fish also attracted interest because they would bring riches when sold in Europe.

Home, Sweet Home

Some of the first colonists who arrived in the New World in 1620 on the Mayflower were hoping to start a new life where they could practice religious freedom. Others were emigrants who hoped to find treasure and eventually go back to England. William Bradford, who was the governor of Plymouth Colony, called them Pilgrims. The Mayflower Compact was the first form of government to be established in the New World. The first winter was very difficult for the Pilgrims. The cold and food shortages caused about half of them to die. By 1627, the colony was established and able to survive.

Colonization

The Massachusetts Bay Colony was founded when John Winthrop came with 1,000 Puritans in 1630. The Puritans did not wish to leave the Church of England, but they did want to change some of its practices. Those who lived in this colony had to follow strict religious ways. You were not allowed to practice your own faith. Eventually the Bay Colony absorbed many of the settlements to form what was know as the British Colony of Massachusetts.

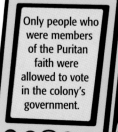

Only people who were members of the Puritan faith were allowed to vote in the colony's government.

Massachusetts Firsts

Massachusetts was ahead of the other colonies for many reasons. Here are a few Massachusetts firsts:

- Celebrated the first Thanksgiving
- Boston Common, first public park
- First public secondary school
- Harvard, first college
- First printing press
- First post office
- Boston Public Library, first major public library
- The Boston Light, the first officially established lighthouse
- First newspaper to be issued regularly
- First ironworks

Massachusetts Firsts

All of these "firsts" happened before the American Revolution!

Legends and Lore

The **Salem witch trials** in 1692 came out of a belief on the part of the Puritans that some people were possessed by the devil. Superstition and fear led to the deaths of at least 19 people in Salem who were accused of witchcraft. During a long boring day in winter, two young girls spent an afternoon with Tituba, a West Indian slave woman, who told them tales of African magic. Eventually more girls came to hear the stories. When fainting spells and fits of crying started, the girls claimed that Tituba had cast a spell on them. This was only the beginning. The frenzy spread! People who held grudges against others would accuse them of witchcraft. There was mob hysteria! Others outside of Salem were also brought to trial and hanged. Finally, the Boston authorities stopped the trials. They also released those remaining in jail. Things calmed down and went back to normal, but this was a tragic time in Salem's history.

"The shot heard

Some settlers in the New World felt that England ignored their ideas and concerns. In 1775, the colonies went to war with England. On July 4, 1776, the Declaration of Independence was signed.

Massachusetts was the center for rebellion against the British Parliament who continued to tax the colonies to pay off British war debts. The Sugar Act, Stamp Act, and Townshend Acts were greatly opposed. In 1770, people in Boston rioted, and during the Boston Massacre, five citizens were killed by British soldiers who fired into the crowd. This further enraged the colonists. To calm them, Britain repealed the Townshend Acts. Again in 1773, Britain imposed a Tea Act on the colonies. A group in Boston, dressed as Native Americans, boarded the ship carrying the first tea shipment from England and dumped it all in the sea. Boston harbor was closed, people were required to house British soldiers in their homes, and Massachusetts' charter was revoked.

Revolution

Crispus Attucks, an African-American patriot, was one of the first men killed during the Boston Massacre.

around the world!"

In 1775, the first battles of the American Revolution occurred outside of Boston. While attempting to warn the colonials of the British approach, patriots Paul Revere and William Dawes were arrested in Lexington. Only Dr. Samuel Prescott, who had joined them, made it to Concord to give the alarm. The colonial militia met British forces at Lexington and Concord outside of Boston. Bunker Hill, overlooking Boston Harbor, was lost to the British. Even though Americans did not force the British to leave Boston, they were a reminder to the rest of the colonies to continue to fight! Finally in 1776, General George Washington drove the British out of Boston. The shot heard around the world was symbolic; it represented the right of people to fight for freedom in their own lands.

Revolution

Founding Father, Samuel Adams, spent fifteen years of his life trying to get the colonists to revolt against British rule. "Taxation without representation" was one of his slogans!

The Civil War

Brother

The Civil War was fought between the American states. The argument was over states' rights to make their own decisions, including whether or not to own slaves. Some of the southern states began to secede (leave) the Union. They formed the Confederate States of America.

In 1780, Massachusetts became the first state to end slavery. Many of the people in Massachusetts were abolitionists, and some offered their homes as stops on the Underground Railroad which allowed slaves to escape to Canada. About 150,000 Massachusetts troops participated in the war from 1861 to 1865.

The Civil War

Word Definition

ABOLITIONIST: a person who believed slavery was wrong and should be ended

44

vs. Brother

The Civil War was also called the War Between the States. Soldiers often found themselves fighting against former friends and neighbors, even brother against brother. Those who did survive often went home without an arm, leg, or both, since amputation was the "cure" for most battlefield wounds. More Americans were killed during the Civil War than during World Wars I and II together!

The Civil War

In 1863, the Emancipation Proclamation, given by U.S. President Abraham Lincoln, freed the slaves still under Confederate control. Some slaves became sharecroppers; others went to Northern states to work in factories.

Get It In Writing!

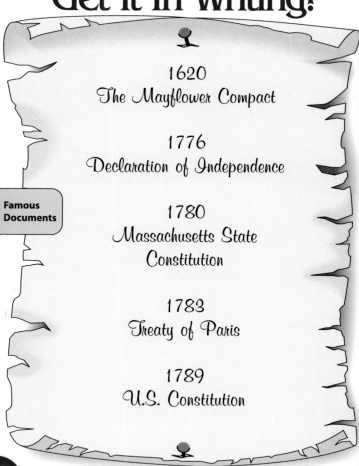

1620
The Mayflower Compact

1776
Declaration of Independence

1780
Massachusetts State
Constitution

1783
Treaty of Paris

1789
U.S. Constitution

WELCOME TO AMERICA!

People have come to Massachusetts from other states and many other countries on almost every continent! As time goes by, Massachusetts' population grows more diverse. This means that people of different races and from different cultures and ethnic backgrounds have moved to Massachusetts.

Immigrants

In the past, many immigrants have come to Massachusetts from Ireland, Poland, Italy, Russia, Greece, Germany, Portugal, Slovakia, Scandinavia, and Canada. More recently, people have migrated to Massachusetts from the Caribbean: Cuba, Haiti, Dominican Republic, and Puerto Rico. Only a certain number of immigrants are allowed to move to America each year. Many of these immigrants eventually become U.S. citizens.

1872

Sixty-five acres in the heart of
Boston destroyed by fire

1919

Boston's Great Molasses Flood, 21 people killed and
150 injured when a two-million ton (1.8 million
metric ton) tank of molasses exploded

1938

Great Hurricane kills
approximatley 600 people in
New England

1942

A fire at the Cocoanut Grove in
Boston kills almost 500 people

1978

A blizzard kills 29 people and causes
one billion dollars in damage

1647

Massachusetts establishes a
public education system

1783

Quork Walker, a slave, sues his master for abuse; state Supreme
Court declares Walker a free man and fines his master

1807

Embargo Act ends trade; destroys
Massachusetts shipping industry

Legal Stuff

1869

Nation's first state board of health is
established in Massachusetts

1910

W.E.B. Dubois founds National Association for
the Advancement of Colored People (NAACP)

1977

Fifty years after execution for robbery and
murder, Nicola Sacco and Bartolomeo Vanzetti
are proclaimed innocent by Governor Dukakis

Women

Poet

Phillis Wheatley was the first published African-American poet in the U.S. In the 1760s she began writing at the age of thirteen while she was still a slave. She was encouraged to write by the family who owned her and eventually was given her freedom.

Soldier

Deborah Sampson joined the army to fight against the British in the American Revolution. She was disguised as a man. In 1983, she was recognized officially as state heroine.

Women

Author

Louisa May Alcott grew up in Boston and was the author of *Little Women,* as well as other popular novels.

Reformer

Susan B. Anthony was a social reformer who worked in the abolition and temperance movements. She won acclaim for all of her effort for women's suffrage. The Susan B. Anthony silver dollar was minted in 1979 in her honor.

Cabinet Member

Frances Perkins became the first female secretary of labor when Franklin D. Roosevelt appointed her in 1933.

Wars

Fight! Fight! Fight!
The wars that Bay Staters participated in are:

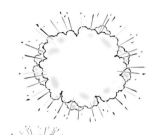

- **King George's War**

- **King William's War**

- **Queen Anne's War**

- **King Philip's War**

- **French and Indian War**

- **Revolutionary War**

Wars

- **Shay's Rebellion**

- **War of 1812**

- **Civil War**

- **World War I**

- **World War II**

- **Korean War**

- **Vietnam War**

- **Persian Gulf War**

Claim to Fame

Extra, Extra, Read All About 'em!

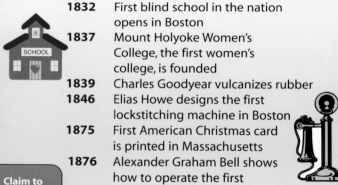

1832	First blind school in the nation opens in Boston
1837	Mount Holyoke Women's College, the first women's college, is founded
1839	Charles Goodyear vulcanizes rubber
1846	Elias Howe designs the first lockstitching machine in Boston
1875	First American Christmas card is printed in Massachusetts
1876	Alexander Graham Bell shows how to operate the first telephone in Boston
1881	Clara Barton founds the American Red Cross
1891	James Naismith of Springfield invents basketball
1893	The Duryea Brothers create the first successful gas-powered automobile in Springfield
1897	Boston has the first subway system in the U.S.

Claim to Fame

Indian Tribes

Algonquian-speaking tribes: Wampanoag, Nauset Massachuset, Nipmuc, Pocumtuc, Pennacook, Mahican

The tribes that inhabited Massachusetts were primarily farmers and hunters. Each tribe lived in different sections of the state. Women had important roles in their society. They owned the land, and when a young man married, he went to live with his bride's family. An Algonquian's ancestry was traced through his mother's side of the family rather than through his father's family.

Indian Tribes

Corn and beans were the Algonquian's main crops. Legend has it that a crow from the Great Father in the southwest brought them a kernel of corn and a bean seed with which to start their garden. They also grew pumpkins and squash.

The Indians of Massachusetts could not have known that the coming of the white man would mean an end to the way of life they had known for hundreds of years.

Here, There, Everywhere!

Leif Ericson—a Viking adventurer, may have landed on Cape Cod as early as AD 1000

John Cabot—an Italian sailing for England; believed to have visited Massachusetts in 1498

Giovanni da Verrazzano—sailed for the French; in 1524 he traced the coastline of Massachusetts

Bartholomew Gosnold—in 1602, he explored around Cape Cod; he built a fort on Cuttyhunk in Buzzards Bay

John Smith—from the Virginia colony, mapped Massachusetts Bay in 1614 and gave many locations their names

Explorers and Colonists

Pilgrims—arrived 1620 on the Mayflower; Mayflower Compact was drawn up; John Carver was elected first governor of Plymouth Colony

Puritans—arrived in 1630 with 1,000 on board the Arbella: John Winthrop was their religious and political leader

Bon Voyage!

N
W   E
S

State Founders

These people played especially important roles in Massachusetts.

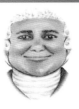

Founding Fathers

William Bradford—took over as governor of Plymouth Colony in 1621; remained governor for over 20 years

John Winthrop—leader of the Puritans; established the Massachusetts Bay colony

Samuel Adams—member of the First and Second Continental Congress; became governor of Massachusetts

Benjamin Franklin—writer, inventor, and diplomat; he helped to negotiate the Paris Peace Treaty in 1783

John Adams—helped draft the Declaration of Independence; first vice-president under Washington

John Hancock—member of the Continental Congress; first man to sign the Declaration of Independence

Founding Mothers

State Founders

Anne Hutchinson—banned from the Puritan colony because of her criticism of their religious beliefs

Mercy Otis Warren—attacked the British in her writings published in the *Massachusetts Spy*

Lydia Child—founder of the first periodical for children and author of an 1800's antislavery book that attracted many to the abolitionist cause

Dorothea Dix—first to study prison conditions; organized the first Army Nursing Corps in 1861

Daughters of St. Crispin—first women's national labor organization; held founding convention in Lynn in 1869

Famous African-Americans

Marie Stuart—having escaped slavery traveled throughout the U.S. speaking out against slavery and for racial justice

Elizabeth Freeman—in 1781 as a slave sued for freedom using the state constitution to challenge slavery; she won, setting a precedent for all future cases in the state

Frederick Douglass—often called "the father of the civil rights movement"; he wrote about his life under slavery and continued to speak out against it all during the 1850s

Famous African-Americans

Sojourner Truth—an escaped slave from Michigan, gave antislavery lectures and worked toward freeing all slaves

Lewis H. Latimer—inventor; he worked with Bell on some of his drawings; member of Edison's Pioneers, a group of Edison's colleagues

Edward William Brooks—elected to the U.S. Senate in 1960; first black U.S. Senator elected since the 1860s

DID SOMEONE SAY BOO!?

A Haunting Review!

Located in Boston, Fort Warren is believed to be haunted by Lieutenant Lanier's wife. The fort was a prison where 600 Confederate soldiers were held. She accidentally shot her husband while trying to help them escape. He died from the wound. Mrs. Lanier was hanged by Union soldiers. They say you can see her footprints in the snow. The sound of rocks rolling along the floor can be heard, and there are other strange phenomena!

Ghosts

DO YOU BELIEVE IN GHOSTS?

Sports Stuff

Rocky Marciano—boxer who won the heavyweight championship in 1952; won all 49 of his bouts; 43 were knockouts

Bill Russell—Boston Celtics center, was pro-basketball's Most Valuable Player five times; first black coach of a pro-sports team

Babe Ruth—Boston Red Sox pitcher until he was traded to the New York Yankees in 1918; the Red Sox have never won a world series since that time (Could it be the Curse of the Bambino?)

Ted Williams—Boston Red Sox outfielder, greatest baseball player, nicknamed the "Splendid Splinter"; one of the best batters of all time

Larry Bird—Boston Celtics forward, sports legend in basketball for his scoring and leadership ability

Jimmie Pedro—participated in the 2000 Sydney Olympics in Judo; came in 5th

Carol Ann Skricki—Summer Olympics 2000 Sydney; came in 4th in double skulls rowing competition

Samantha Arsenault—4x200 freestyle relay in swimming; won the gold medal

Kara Wolters—was part of the Olympic Dream Team III; took the gold in basketball at Sydney 2000 Olympics

Leonard Bernstein—great conductor and composer; wrote *West Side Story*

Bette Davis—actress who won Academy Awards for *Dangerous* and *Jezebel*

Jack Lemmon—actor, starred in *The Odd Couple* and *Grumpy Old Men*; won an Oscar for *Mister Roberts* and *Save the Tiger*

Serge Koussevitzky—Russian-born primary conductor of the Boston Symphony Orchestra 1924–1949

Jane Alexander—won a Tony Award for her performance in *The Great White Hope*; was head of the National Endowment for the Arts in 1993

Leonard Nemoy—actor, portrayed Dr. Spock in *Star Trek*

Arthur Fiedler—conducted Boston Pops Orchestra for almost 50 years

Sarah Caldwell—Boston Opera Company, first woman to conduct a major orchestra

Armando "Chick" Corea—keyboard player and composer; Grammy Award winner; combines different types of music

Entertainers

Authors

Anne Bradstreet—English colonist; in 1650, she wrote the first published book of poetry in the colonies

Louisa May Alcott—author of *Little Women* and *Little Men*

Edgar Allan Poe—wrote scary poems and stories; earned reputation as nation's finest horror writer

Theodore Seuss Geisel—Dr. Seuss, wrote rhyming books about make-believe characters

Ralph Waldo Emerson—philosopher, minister, essayist and poet

Julia Ward Howe—social reformer and author; wrote the text of the "Battle Hymn of the Republic"

Henry Wadsworth Longfellow—most beloved poet of 19th century

Henry David Thoreau—essayist, naturalist,and philosopher, isolated himself at Walden Pond writing and studying about nature

John Greenleaf Whittier—known as the "Quaker Poet"; wrote about his boyhood in New England

Emily Dickinson—one of America's finest poets

Anne Sexton—poet and professor, won Pulitzer Prize in poetry 1967

Amy Lowell—poet, critic, and lecturer, won Pulitzer Prize in 1926 in poetry for *What's O'Clock*

Riddle? What do you get when something completely disappears? Quoth The Raven: "Nevermore!"

Artists

YOU GOTTA HAVE ART!

Winslow Homer—self-taught artist, best known for his seascapes

N. C. Wyeth—illustrator of children's books such as *Treasure Island* and *Robin Hood*

John Singleton Copley—considered the finest portrait artist of his time

Daniel Chester French—sculptor; created Lincoln statue in the Lincoln Memorial in Washington, D.C.

James Abbott McNeill Whistler—artist, painted famous *Whistler's Mother* portrait

John Singer Sargent—artist, painted water colors and murals

Albert Pinkham Ryder—painted the sea; sentimental in his artistic approach

William Morris Hunt—influenced others with his interest in the Barbizon school in France

Ralph and Martha Cahoon—primitive artists, opened the Cahoon Museum of Art in 1984

Harriet Goodhue Hosmer— sculptor who did busts and classical figures; studied in Rome

Katharine Murphy Jenness—charcoal portrait artist; does charcoals outdoors on Bearskin Neck

Eli Whitney—invented the cotton gin; made the U.S. a world leader in the production of cotton in the 1800s

Samuel Morse—invented the telegraph and Morse code

Alexander Graham Bell—Boston, invented the telephone; taught at Boston University

Elias Howe—invented the modern sewing machine in the 1840s

Percival Lowell—helped to discover the planet, Pluto

Mary Baker Eddy—founded daily newspaper *The Christian Science Monitor*

Horace Mann—referred to as the father of American public education; led the fight for free, universal education

Very Important People

Lucy Stone—abolitionist; organized the American Woman Suffrage Association in 1869

Edwin Land—produced the first instant-picture camera; he was second only to Thomas Edison regarding the number of patents he had on his inventions

Frederick Law Olmsted—19th century landscape architect, designed New York's Central Park and six parks in Boston called the "Emerald Necklace"

More Very Important People

Mary Lyon—founded the first women's college in the country, Mount Holyoke Female Seminary

Oliver Wendell Holmes—physician, educator, author; taught at Harvard Medical School for over 30 years; helped start the *Atlantic Monthly* magazine

Milton Bradley—inventor of board games; his company is the oldest and largest manufacturer of games

Isabella Stewart Gardner—patron of painters, literary figures, musicians, and others; the Isabella Stewart Gardner Museum is part of her mansion and houses many famous pieces of art

John Harvard—left half his estate and a 400-volume library to the new college at Cambridge; the school was named in his honor

William Lloyd Garrison—journalist and reformer; founded the American Anti-Slavery Society

Francis Cabot Lowell—founded the first textile firm that turned raw cotton into cloth

Political Leaders

John Adams—vice president under Washington; 2nd president of the U.S.

John Quincy Adams—John's son; became the the 6th president

Daniel Webster—most famous orator of his time; U.S. representative and senator; secretary of state under three presidents

Calvin Coolidge—governor of Massachusetts; vice president under Harding; 30th president of the U.S.

John Fitzgerald Kennedy—35th president; U.S. representative and senator; established the Peace Corps in 1961; worked for civil rights reform, manned space flights, and social welfare programs; was assassinated by Lee Harvey Oswald in Dallas, Texas, in 1963

Political Leaders

Edward Moore Kennedy—U.S. senator since 1962; consistently supports civil rights and social reform legislation

Robert Francis Kennedy—U.S. attorney general; U.S. senator from New York; assassinated in 1968 while campaigning in Los Angeles

George Herbert Walker Bush—born in Milton; 41st president of U.S.; vice president under Ronald Reagan; George Walker Bush, the 43rd president, is his son

Freedom Trail

Freedom Trail is a walking tour in downtown Boston that points out the major landmarks of the city during Colonial and Revolutionary times. Marks of red on the sidewalk indicate the specific sites. Granary Burying Ground has the graves of famous leaders like Samuel Adams. The first free public school is marked, and there is a statue of Benjamin Franklin nearby. One of the oldest buildings in the city is the Old Globe Corner Bookstore built in 1712. The Old State House, built in 1729, was where the royal governor and colonial legislature met. The Boston Massacre took place right outside. In 1776, the Declaration of Independence was first read to the citizens of the city from the balcony. Faneuil Hall was a gathering place for meetings just prior to the American Revolution. Paul Revere's home is marked and so is the Old North Church. Across the Charles River are two more landmarks: the Battle of Bunker Hill, and the USS *Constitution*, *Old Ironsides*.

Freedom Trail

Keeping the Faith

King's Chapel, Boston—first church of Unitarian denomination after the Revolution

Old North Church, Boston—originally an Anglican church, the steeple was used to signal that the British were coming at the beginning of the Revolutionary War

Christ Church, Cambridge—the oldest Anglican church there, used by the Americans during the Revolutionary War as a barracks

West Parish Congregational Church, Barnstable—1634, oldest Congregational parish in the nation

Cataumet Methodist Church, Bourne—was built in 1765 for the Native American congregation

SCHOOLS

Harvard University, Cambridge—founded in 1636, first college in the country

Massachusetts Institute of Technology, Cambridge—one of the nation's top science and engineering schools

University of Massachusetts, Amherst—the state's largest university system, also has branches in Boston and Worcester

Smith College, Northampton—founded for women in 1875

Williams College, Williamstown—named for Colonel Ephraim Williams who left in his will a bequest to found the town and a free school

Churches and Schools

HISTORIC SITES

Salem Maritime National Historic Site—waterfront wharves and buildings from the time when Salem was a busy seaport

Black Heritage Trail, Boston—walking tour, explores history of the 19th century Beacon Hill African-American community

Sleepy Hollow Cemetery, Concord—contains the graves of Thoreau, Emerson, Hawthorne and other famous people of the state

Springfield Armory—founded 1777; used for the manufacture of weapons

PARKS

Boston National Historic Park—covers 41 acres (17 hectares) including the "Freedom Tail"

Longfellow Historic Park, Cambridge—home of Henry Wadsworth Longfellow for 45 years, where he wrote his famous poetry

Lowell National Historic Park—site of the first planned industrial city in the U.S.; named after Francis Cabot Lowell

Home, Sweet Home!

★ EARLY RESIDENCY

Beacon Hill, Boston—preserved 19th century district; highest elevation in Boston; once home to the elite of the city; full of architectural and historic treasures

Ralph Waldo Emerson House, Concord—built by the writer; where he lived until his death in 1882

Old Manse, Concord—home of Ralph Waldo Emerson; later lived in by Nathaniel Hawthorne

Witch House, Salem—restored 17th century house; once the home of Jonathan Corwin, a witchcraft-trial judge

Orchard House, Concord— The home of Louisa May Alcott's family

Plimoth Plantation, Plymouth—re-created as an original 1627 Pilgrim village

Frederick Law Olmsted National Historic Site, Brookline—home and office of the famous 19th century landscape architect

John F. Kennedy National Historic Site, Brookline—birthplace of the 35th president of the U.S.

Old Sturbridge Village—200 acres (81 hectares) with a re-creation of a rural 19th century New England community

Paul Revere's House, Boston—only remaining 17th century structure in the city

Battles and Forts

A few of Massachusetts' famous Battles

● **Minute Man National Historical Park, Lexington and Concord**—site of first battles of the Revolution, famous statue, *The Minute Man,* is there along with a reconstructed North Bridge where the minutemen stood their ground against the British; five mile Battle Road is also within the park area

● **Breed's Hill, Charlestown**—in 1775 the British attacked the fortification; Americans were forced to retreat to Bunker Hill

● **Bunker Hill, Boston**—American's fall-back entrenchment; battle lost to the British who had twice as many casualties

A few of Massachusetts' famous Forts

● **Fort Hill Preserve, Eastham**— the remains of an early Pilgrim settlement with stone walls and remnants of house sites

● **Fort Independence, Castle Island**—star-shaped, massive fortification completed in 1851, fired upon by the colonists; eventually was evacuated by the British

● **Fort Warren, Boston Harbor**—built during the 1830s; housed Confederate prisoners during the Civil War

Libraries

Check out the following special Massachusetts libraries! (Do you have a library card? Have you worn it out yet?!)

Boston Public Library—nation's oldest major library, founded 1854

Worcester Public Library, 850,000 volumes

Harvard University library system, Cambridge—nearly 10 million volumes, largest and one of the best library systems in the world

John Fitzgerald Kennedy Library, Dorchester—houses papers and other memorabilia of the 35th president

Boston Athenaeum—best known private library in the state

Worcester's American Antiquarian Society has the world's largest collection of early newspapers, children's books, sheet music, and other printed materials.

Zoos and Attractions

Walden Pond, Concord—Henry David Thoreau's cabin is there; visitors can picnic, swim, and fish

Kendall Whaling Museum, Cohasset—history of whaling worldwide

Salt Pond Visitors Center of Cape Cod National Seashore—vistas of the salt ponds and coastline

Swan Boats, Boston—float around the lagoon at the Public Garden in a pedal-powered boat

Arcadia Nature Center and Wildlife Sanctuary, Easthampton—hawk watches, wildflower walks

Berkshire Botanic Gardens, Stockbridge—massive daylilies, wild flowers, herbs, and shrubs

Fenway Victory Gardens, Boston—small plots holding vegetables and flowers during the growing season

Pleasant Valley Wildlife Sanctuary—beaver dams and lodges, natural history museum

Wachusett Meadow Wildlife Sanctuary—Massachusetts Audubon property, observation platforms for viewing plants and animals

Zoos and Attractions

LION

Museums

John F. Kennedy Hyannis Museum—photography of the young Kennedy family

Hancock Shaker Village, Pittsfield—learn about Shaker history while touring the community that existed here

The Henry N. Flynt Silverwork and Metal Collection, Deerfield—displays of English and American silver and pewter; some items by Paul Revere

Hull Lifesaving Museum—traces the history of brave surfmen and devastating shipwrecks

Custom House Maritime Museum, Newburyport—birthplace of the U.S. Coast Guard; houses much maritime memorabilia

New Bedford Whaling Museum, New Bedford—holds world's largest ship model, 89 foot (27 meter) *Lagoda*

Wampanoag Indian Museum, Mashpee—collection of Native American artifacts from their encampment; the Wampanoag introduced cranberries to the Pilgrims

Museums

Lest We Forget

MONUMENTS and MEMORIALS

Plymouth Rock Monument—where Pilgrims first stepped ashore to settle, replica of their vessel, the *Mayflower II,* nearby

Statue of Paul Revere, Boston—Paul Revere Mall; a public park, statue has Revere upon a horse

Lexington Green's Revolutionary War Monument—erected 1799

Old Granary Burying Ground, Boston—many Founding Fathers buried there, including three signers of the Declaration of Independence

Cheshire Cheese Monument—replica of a cider press that was used to make a 1,235-pound (560-kilogram) cheese which was sent to President Jefferson in 1802 by the townspeople

Pilgrim Monument, Cape Cod—to commemorate their landing first in Provincetown; tallest granite structure in the U.S., 252 feet (77 meters) tall

Monuments
and
Memorials

Bunker Hill Monument, Charlestown—tallest monolith erected in the U.S. until the Washington Monument in 1885

Calvin Coolidge Memorial Room, Amherst—Forbes Library, contains family remembrances

Roger Conant Statue, Salem—founder, stands in front of the Witch Museum

The Arts

The Busch-Reisinger Museum, Harvard—one of three Harvard art museums, houses collections of Central and Northern European art

Worcester Art Museum—one of New England's finest collections of American paintings

Sterling and Francine Clark Art Institute, Williamstown—one of the finest small museums in the country

George Walter Vincent Smith Art Museum, Springfield—houses Japanese arms, Chinese cloisonne, Oriental jades, textiles, and ceramics

Museum of Fine Arts, Springfield—has centuries of art, impressionists, expressionists, and early European paintings

Museum of Fine Arts, Boston—founded 1870, contains paintings, sculpture, furniture, and decorative arts; best collection of Asian art in the Western Hemisphere

The Arts

Art Complex Museum, Duxbury—Asian art, Shaker, and American works

Fogg Art Museum, Cambridge—holds master paintings by van Gogh, Renoir, Rubens, and others

To be or not to be involved in the arts—that is the question. What is your answer?

Lighthouses

BY THE LIGHT . . .

Gurnet Point, Plymouth Harbor—twin lighthouses, used by colonists as landmarks to guide them into safe harbors; Hannah Thomas was the first female lighthouse keeper in the colonies

Chatham Light, Cape Cod—Angeline Nickerson, keeper, 1848–1859

Lighthouse Point, Scituate—during the War of 1812, legend has it that two little girls scared off a British man-of-war by beating pots and pans together at the Point

Highland Light, Cape Cod—at one time, it was one of the most powerful Atlantic coast lights

Sankatay Head Lighthouse, Nantucket—has warned ships off the shoals since 1861

Gay Head Light, Martha's Vineyard—available for touring mid-June through September, very beautiful view of surrounding area

Great Point Lighthouse, Nantucket—one of three lighthouses located on the island

Lighthouses

Roads,

King's Highway, route 6A runs along the north shore of Cape Cod—no one knows which king ordered it built in the 1700s
Commonwealth Avenue, Boston—modeled after Parisian boulevards; it is 240 feet (74 meters) wide with a green mall running up the center with statues and trees; residential properties and private clubs are along the avenue

Bridges,

Bridge of Sighs, between Beacon Hill and Back Bay—designed by William Prescott in the late 19th century in the Public Garden; many couples have courted here giving it the nickname, "Bridge of Sighs"
North Bridge, Concord—commemorative bridge was rebuilt on the site once in 1875, and again in 1956
Sagamore and Bourne Bridges, Cape Cod—built over the Cape Cod Canal; won an award for being "the most beautiful steel bridges" when they were finished in 1935

Roads, Bridges, and More!

and More!

Cape Cod Canal—opened in 1914; 17-mile (27-kilometer) canal saves seamen the 100-mile (161-kilometer) trip around the Cape
Martha's Vineyard & Nantucket Steamship Authority—provides auto and passenger service year-round going to and from the islands
The Emerald Necklace, Boston—a green 5-mile (8-kilometer) stretch that links the parks that Frederick Law Olmsted designed for the city

Swamps, Bogs, and Marshes

Squam Swamp, Nantucket—project of the Conservation Foundation; geological and natural history are featured along a one-mile (1.61-kilometer) walk through the swamp

Parker River National Wildlife Refuge, Plum Island—sand, beaches, dunes, bogs tidal marshes, and ponds; over 800 species of birds, plants, and animals

Essex River Basin—marshes, estuaries, and saltwater creeks

Cape Cod Museum of Natural History, Chatham—82-acre (33-hectare) grounds; three nature trails are available with wetlands and salt marsh to the beach

Nauset Marsh, Cape Cod—protected marshland and estuaries covering 30 square miles (78 square kilometers); best explored by kayak or canoe

Swamps, Bogs, and Marshes

Gee, do they make bug spray for Lady bugs?

I sure hope so! The mosquitoes in the swamp will be too much for me!

MASSACHUSETTS' ANIMALS INCLUDE:

Deer
Bats
Beavers
Chipmunks
Meadow Mice
Foxes
Moles
Raccoons
Muskrats
Porcupines
Rabbits
Shrews
Bears
Skunks
Snakes
Squirrels
Coyotes
Weasels
Woodchucks

Animals

Muskrats like a habitat that is wet. Marshes,
edges of ponds, lakes, streams, and open water
are some of their favorite places to live.

Take a Walk on the Wild Side!

Some endangered Massachusetts' animals are:

Blue Whale
Fin Whale
Humpback Whale
Northern Right Whale
Sperm Whale
Stormy Petrel
Bald Eagle
Peregrine Falcon
Sedge Wren
Short-eared Owl
Roseate Tern
Golden-winged Warbler
Bog Turtle
Copperhead
Timber Rattlesnake
Plymouth Redbelly Turtle

Some of the early sailors involved in the whaling trade used to make carvings called *scrimshaw* out of whale bone or teeth.

Wildlife Watch

Birds

You may spy these birds in Massachusetts

Chickadees
Blue Jays
Cardinals
Mallard Ducks
Grouse
Gulls
Bald Eagles
Mockingbirds
Owls
Partridges
Pheasant
Quails
Terns
Woodpeckers
Hummingbirds

A hummingbird's wings beat 75 times a second—so fast that you only see a blur! They make short squeaky sounds, but do not sing.

Birds

Insects

Don't let these Massachusetts bugs bug you!

Buckeyes
Butterflies
Underwings
Moths
Crickets
Katydids
Walking Sticks
May Beetles
Japanese Beetles
Sphinx Moths
Whirligig Beetles

Honeybee

Butterfly

Dragon Fly

Praying Mantis

Firefly

Ladybug

Grasshopper

Do we know any of these bugs?

Maybe... Hey, that ladybug is cute!

Whirligig beetles have two pairs of eyes—one pair looks above the water, the other under it!

Water Creatures

Pollock
Flounder
Haddock
Cod
Smelt
Striped Bass
Blue Fish
Clams
Scallops
Lobster

Water
Creatures

Pond Critters

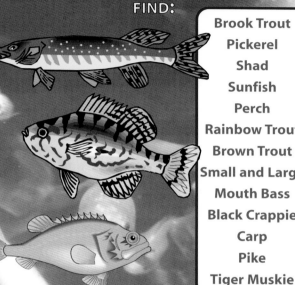

- Brook Trout
- Pickerel
- Shad
- Sunfish
- Perch
- Rainbow Trout
- Brown Trout
- Small and Large Mouth Bass
- Black Crappie
- Carp
- Pike
- Tiger Muskie

The brook trout flourishes in water less than 50°F (10°C). It can weigh about 2 pounds (0.91 kilograms) or more.

Pond Critters

Seashells

She sells seashells by the Massachusetts seashore!

Chitons
Top Shells
Periwinkles
Slipper Shells
Moon Shells
Wentletraps
Whelks
Vampire Shell
Bubble Shell
Mussels
Scallops
Cockles
Coquina Shells
Angel Shells
Ship Worms

Seashells

There are 200 different varieties of wentletraps. They are usually white in color and can secrete a purple dye.

TREEMENDOUS!

THESE TREES TOWER OVER MASSACHUSETTS:

- AMERICAN ELM
- BLACK WALNUT
- BLACK TUPELO
- AMERICAN SYCAMORE
- SOURWOOD
- SASSAFRAS
- NORTHERN RED OAK
- RED MULBERRY
- RED MAPLE
- EASTERN COTTONWOOD
- HACKBERRY
- AMERICAN HOLLY
- EASTERN REDBUD
- BLACK CHERRY

Trees

Wildflowers

Are you crazy about these **Massachusetts** wildflowers?

Mayflower
Violet
Trillium
Wild Geranium
Jack-in-the-Pulpit
Columbine
Lady's Slipper
Jacob's Ladder
Black-eyed Susan

Buttercup
Goldenrod
Chicory
Queen Ann's Lace
Milkweed
Oxeye Daisy
Lupine
Butter-and-Eggs

Do you ever think you would eat Butter-and-Eggs for a sore throat? Early colonists used this beautiful yellow and orange flower to make a medicine that soothed a scratchy throat!

Flower Power!

Cream of the Crops

Agricultural products from Massachusetts:

Cranberries
Dairy Products
Sheep
Fruit
Scallops
Fish

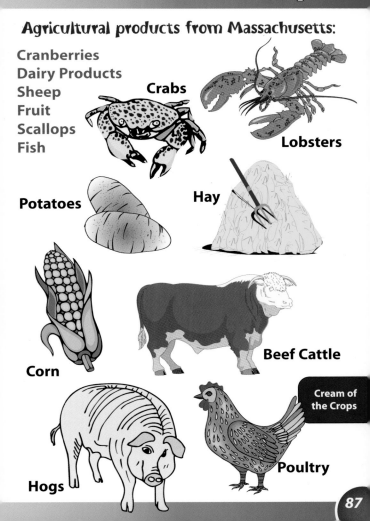

Crabs

Lobsters

Potatoes

Hay

Corn

Beef Cattle

Cream of the Crops

Hogs

Poultry

First/Biggest/Smallest/Etc.

Fenway Park is the **smallest major league baseball** park in the U.S. but has the tallest outfield wall, the Green Monster!

The Boston Celtics have been acclaimed one of the **best sports franchises** of all time.

The textile industry was the **most important industry** in Massachusetts for about 100 years during the 19th and early 20th centuries.

Boston is part of a **megalopolis** that runs throughout northeastern Massachusetts.

Boston is sometimes called **the Hub** by Bay Staters.

Several well-known men and women in the state were part of the **transcendental movement** during the 19th century which had its focus on free-thinking and the questioning of religious beliefs. They worked toward more social reform.

Thousands of tourists come to Cape Cod each year. Sandwich is the **oldest town** on the cape.

Whale-watching cruises are a very **popular attraction.**

Every town in Massachusetts has a **public library**, and most have a historical museum.

The Wampanoag people taught the early colonists how to make **pemmican** out of venison and cranberries.

First/
Biggest/
Smallest/Ect.

Festivals

Tanglewood Art Festival, Lenox

Williamstown Theater Festival

Jacob's Pillow Dance Festival, Lee

New England Spring Flower Show, Boston

Daffodil Festival, Nantucket Island

Cambridge River Festival

Up-Country Hot Air Balloon Fair, Greenfield

Blessing of the Fishing Fleets, Gloucester and Provincetown

Harborfest, Boston

Cranberry Festival, Harwick

World Kielbasa Festival, Chicopee

Scallop Festival, Buzzards Bay

Rowing Regatta, Charles River in Boston and Cambridge

Haunted Happenings, Salem

Cape Cod Chowder Festival, Hyannis

Holidays
Calendar

Martin Luther King, Jr. Day, *3rd Monday in January*	Presidents' Day, *3rd Monday in February*	Boston Saint Patrick's Day Parade, *Sunday before March 17*
Boston Marathon, *3rd Monday in April*	Memorial Day, *last Monday in May*	Bunker Hill Day, Charlestown *June 17*
Independence Day, *July 4*	Labor Day, *1st Monday in September*	Columbus Day, *2nd Monday in October*
Veterans Day, *November 11*	Thanksgiving, *4th Thursday in November*	

Christmas, Chanukah, Kwanzaa, Vietnamese Tet, and Chinese New Year are all special celebrations in Massachusetts.

Massachusetts celebrates Ratification Day on February 6.

Famous Food

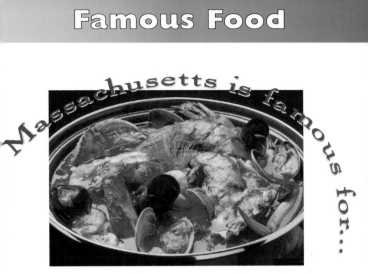

Massachusetts is famous for...

the following foods!

Pasta	Boston Baked Beans	Kielbasa
Pizza	Lobster	*Pierogi*
Oysters	Cod	Rice Pudding
Figs	Crab Cakes	Irish Bread
Duck	Clams	*Golabki*
Sushi	Cornbeef and Cabbage	Steak and
Stir-fry	Cranberries	Kidney Pie

Yum, yum. This is great!

Let's dig in!

Massachusetts Works!

Massachusetts has a diverse economy with several major industries that produce electrical and electronic equipment, textiles and shoes, processed foods, paper and paper products, plastics, and tools. The Boston area from Braintree to Gloucester has been called the Golden Semicircle because so many high-tech companies are located there. More and more software development and bioresearch are being done.

The service industries account for about a third of the work force in the state. Health care, education, law, computer programming, and engineering are just some of the career choices people are making. Another 44 percent work in wholesale and retail trade, government, finance, insurance, or real estate.

Boston has two of the nation's largest banks headquartered there. It is a major financial center.

Business & Trade

My First Book About Massachusetts
by Carole Marsh
America the Beautiful: Massachusetts
by Sylvia McNair
Kids Learn America
by Patricia Gordon and Reed C. Snow
From Sea to Shining Sea: Massachusetts
by Dennis Brindell Fradin
Let's Discover the States: Massachusetts
by the Aylesworths
The Massachusetts Experience Series
by Carole Marsh

COOL MASSACHUSETTS WEBSITES

http://www.state.ma.us
http://www.massachusettsexperience.com
http://www.50states.com
http://www.netstate.com

Massachusetts
Glossary

GLOSSARY WORDS

bog: wet, spongy ground, a small marsh or swamp

bivalve: a water animal whose soft body is inside a shell of two parts hinged together; examples: clams and oysters

emigrants: people who leave one country to settle in another

grudge: to envy a person because of what that person has

hibernate: to spend the winter in a kind of sleep

megalopolis: a very large, crowded area made up of many cities

minutemen: members of the American citizen army at the time of the Revolutionary War

surfmen: men who went out to rescue those caught in storms at sea

transcendentalism: nothing is as it seems to appear, a philosophy where intuition is the key to understanding reality

Massachusetts

Spelling Bee

Here are some special Massachusetts-related words to learn! To take the Spelling Bee, have someone call out the words and you spell them aloud or write them on a piece of paper.

SPELLING WORDS

American	Massachusetts
Berkshire	minutemen
Boston	patriot
Cambridge	pemmican
colonial	Pilgrim
cranberries	Puritans
declaration	revolution
Harvard	surfmen
Housatonic	suffrage
Lexington	textiles

Spelling List

ABOUT THE AUTHOR...

CAROLE MARSH has been writing about Massachusetts for more than 20 years. She is the author of the popular *Massachusetts State Stuff Series* for young readers and creator along with her son, Michael Marsh, of *Massachusetts Facts and Factivities*, a CD-ROM widely used in Massachusetts schools. The author of more than 100 Massachusetts books and other supplementary educational materials on the state, Marsh is currently working on a new collection of Massachusetts materials for young people. Marsh correlates her Massachusetts materials to the Massachusetts learning standards. Many of her books and other materials have been inspired by or requested by Massachusetts teachers and librarians.

You know... that was a great experience!

Sure was! Thanks for taking me along.

EDITORIAL ASSISTANT AND FORMER BAY STATER:
Jackie Clayton

GRAPHIC DESIGNER:
Lisa Stanley